Table Of Contents

01

Chapter 1: Introduction to AI in Video Production

The Rise of AI in Video Production

In recent years, the integration of artificial intelligence (AI) in video production has revolutionized the way content creators approach their craft. AI technologies have drastically improved the efficiency and quality of video production processes, offering a wide range of tools and techniques that were previously unimaginable. This subchapter will explore the various ways in which AI is transforming the landscape of video production and how content creators can leverage these advancements to enhance their work.

One of the most significant contributions of AI to video production is the development of AI-driven video editing techniques. These tools utilize machine learning algorithms to automate and streamline the editing process, enabling creators to achieve professional-level results in a fraction of the time. From color correction to audio syncing, AI-powered editing tools have become essential in maximizing efficiency and improving the overall quality of video content.

Additionally, AI-powered video enhancement tools have become invaluable assets for content creators looking to elevate the visual appeal of their videos. These tools utilize advanced algorithms to enhance image quality, reduce noise, and optimize lighting conditions, resulting in visually stunning videos that captivate audiences. Whether it's enhancing the sharpness of an image or removing unwanted elements from a scene, AI-powered enhancement tools have become essential in elevating the production value of video content.

Moreover, AI applications in virtual reality video production have opened up new possibilities for immersive storytelling and interactive experiences. By leveraging AI algorithms, content creators can create hyper-realistic virtual environments, enhance spatial audio, and improve the overall user experience in virtual reality videos. With the integration of AI, virtual reality video production has become more accessible and engaging, offering audiences a truly immersive viewing experience like never before.

Furthermore, AI in live video streaming and production has revolutionized the way events are broadcasted and consumed by audiences worldwide. AI-powered tools can automate camera movements, adjust audio levels, and optimize video quality in real-time, ensuring a seamless viewing experience for viewers. Whether it's a live concert, sporting event, or corporate presentation, AI-driven live video production tools have become essential in delivering high-quality, engaging content to audiences in real-time.

In conclusion, the rise of AI in video production has ushered in a new era of creativity, efficiency, and innovation for content creators. From automated editing techniques to advanced enhancement tools, AI technologies have transformed the way videos are produced, enhancing the overall quality and impact of content. As the capabilities of AI continue to evolve, the possibilities for AI-driven video production are limitless, offering content creators an array of tools and techniques to create compelling, immersive, and engaging videos for audiences worldwide.

Why AI is Revolutionizing the Industry

Artificial Intelligence (AI) has completely revolutionized the video production industry in recent years, offering innovative solutions to streamline workflows and enhance the overall quality of content. With the integration of AI-driven video editing techniques, production teams are able to automate mundane tasks such as color correction, audio syncing, and even scene selection. This not only saves time and resources but also allows creators to focus on the creative aspects of their projects.

In addition to editing, AI-powered video enhancement tools have become increasingly popular among video producers. These tools utilize machine learning algorithms to automatically enhance video quality, remove noise, and even upscale resolution. This ensures that the final product is of the highest possible quality, without the need for manual intervention.

Furthermore, AI applications in virtual reality video production have opened up new possibilities for immersive storytelling. By analyzing user behavior and preferences, AI algorithms can create personalized virtual reality experiences that cater to individual interests. This level of personalization not only enhances user engagement but also allows for more targeted marketing strategies.

AI has also made a significant impact on live video streaming and production, with algorithms able to automatically adjust camera angles, lighting, and audio levels in real-time. This ensures a seamless and professional viewing experience for audiences, regardless of the production environment.

Overall, the integration of AI-driven technologies in video production workflows has not only increased efficiency and productivity but has also enabled creators to push the boundaries of storytelling and audience engagement. As AI continues to evolve, its applications in video production will only become more advanced, offering endless possibilities for innovation and creativity in the industry.

Understanding the Basics of AI Technology

Artificial Intelligence (AI) technology has revolutionized the field of video production in recent years, offering a wide range of tools and techniques that can enhance the quality and efficiency of video editing, enhancement, virtual reality production, live streaming, analytics, content creation, post-production workflows, personalization, automated captioning, translation, and interactive storytelling. Understanding the basics of AI technology is essential for anyone looking to leverage the power of AI in video production effectively.

The Ultimate Guide to AI in Video Production

One of the fundamental aspects of AI technology in video production is its ability to analyze and interpret data automatically. AI algorithms can process vast amounts of video footage, images, and audio files to identify patterns, trends, and insights that humans may overlook. This capability is particularly useful in video analytics, where AI can provide valuable audience insights and help creators make data-driven decisions to optimize their content for maximum engagement.

Another key aspect of AI technology in video production is its capacity for automating repetitive tasks and workflows. AI-powered video editing tools can streamline the editing process by automatically selecting the best shots, applying filters and effects, and even generating rough cuts based on predefined criteria. This automation can save video producers a significant amount of time and effort, allowing them to focus on the creative aspects of their work.

The Ultimate Guide to AI in Video Production

AI technology also plays a crucial role in enhancing the visual and audio quality of videos. AI-powered tools can remove noise, stabilize shaky footage, improve color grading, and even upscale low-resolution videos to higher resolutions. These enhancements can make videos look more professional and polished, ultimately increasing their appeal to viewers and enhancing the overall viewing experience.

In addition to editing and enhancement, AI technology is also being used in virtual reality video production to create immersive and interactive experiences. AI algorithms can analyze user behavior and preferences in real-time to adapt the VR content accordingly, creating personalized experiences that engage and captivate audiences. AI-driven virtual reality production is pushing the boundaries of storytelling and allowing creators to explore new creative possibilities in the medium.

Overall, understanding the basics of AI technology is essential for anyone interested in harnessing its power in video production. By leveraging AI-driven tools and techniques, video producers can enhance the quality of their content, automate repetitive tasks, gain valuable audience insights, create immersive VR experiences, and tell compelling stories in innovative ways. The possibilities are endless, and with a solid understanding of AI technology, the future of video production is sure to be exciting and transformative.

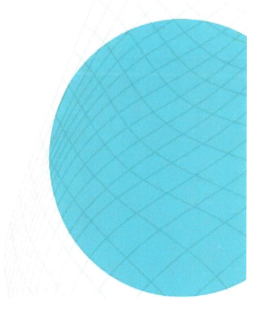

02

Chapter 2:
Comprehensive Guide on
AI in Video Production

AI-powered Video Editing Techniques

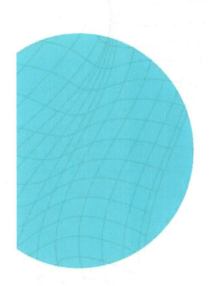

AI-powered video editing techniques have revolutionized the way video content is produced and edited. With the advancements in artificial intelligence technology, video editors now have access to powerful tools that can automate tedious tasks, enhance visual effects, and streamline the editing process. In this subchapter, we will explore some of the AI-driven video editing techniques that are changing the landscape of video production.

One of the most popular AI-powered video editing techniques is automated video tagging and categorization. This technology uses machine learning algorithms to analyze video content and automatically tag scenes based on their content. This saves editors countless hours of manual tagging and allows them to quickly search for specific scenes or subjects within their footage.

Another key AI-driven video editing technique is automated color correction and grading. AI algorithms can analyze the colors in a video and adjust them to create a more visually appealing and cohesive look. This technology can save editors time and ensure that their videos have a professional and polished appearance.

AI-powered video enhancement tools are also becoming increasingly popular in the industry. These tools use artificial intelligence to enhance video quality, reduce noise, and improve overall visual clarity. By using these tools, editors can quickly enhance their videos without the need for manual adjustments.

AI applications in virtual reality video production are also on the rise. Virtual reality videos require complex editing techniques to create immersive experiences for viewers. AI algorithms can help streamline this process by automating tasks such as stitching together multiple camera angles or removing unwanted objects from the scene.

In conclusion, AI-powered video editing techniques are transforming the way video content is produced and edited. From automated tagging and categorization to color correction and grading, AI technology is revolutionizing the industry. By embracing these advancements, video editors can save time, improve the quality of their videos, and create more engaging content for their audiences.

AI-driven Video Enhancement Tools

AI-driven video enhancement tools are revolutionizing the way video content is created and produced. These powerful tools use artificial intelligence algorithms to analyze and enhance video quality, making footage look more professional and polished. From color correction to noise reduction, AI-driven video enhancement tools can improve the overall visual appeal of videos, resulting in a more engaging viewing experience for audiences.

One of the key benefits of using AI-driven video enhancement tools is their ability to automate the editing process, saving time and effort for video producers. By leveraging machine learning algorithms, these tools can quickly identify and correct common issues such as shaky footage, poor lighting, and blurry images. This allows content creators to focus on the creative aspects of video production, rather than getting bogged down in technical details.

In addition to improving video quality, AI-driven video enhancement tools can also help streamline the production workflow. These tools can be integrated into existing editing software, making it easier for video producers to access and apply enhancements to their footage. This level of automation not only speeds up the editing process but also ensures a consistent level of quality across all videos.

Furthermore, AI-driven video enhancement tools are constantly evolving and improving, thanks to ongoing advancements in artificial intelligence technology. As algorithms become more sophisticated and powerful, the capabilities of these tools will continue to expand, allowing video producers to achieve even better results with their content. This ongoing innovation makes AI-driven video enhancement tools a valuable asset for anyone looking to create high-quality videos.

Overall, AI-driven video enhancement tools are a game-changer for the video production industry. By leveraging the power of artificial intelligence, content creators can enhance the visual quality of their videos, streamline the editing process, and stay ahead of the competition. As these tools continue to evolve and improve, they will play an increasingly important role in the future of video production, helping to shape the way content is created and consumed in the digital age.

AI Applications in Virtual Reality Video Production

Virtual reality (VR) has become increasingly popular in recent years, allowing users to immerse themselves in a completely digital environment. With the help of artificial intelligence (AI), the production of VR videos has become more efficient and realistic than ever before. AI algorithms can be used to enhance the quality of VR video content, making the experience more immersive for viewers.

One of the key applications of AI in virtual reality video production is in the creation of realistic 3D environments. AI algorithms can analyze real-world footage and generate 3D models of objects and environments, which can then be used to create immersive VR experiences.

This technology allows content creators to easily create realistic virtual worlds without the need for expensive equipment or extensive technical knowledge.

Another important application of AI in VR video production is in the editing and post-production process. AI-driven video editing techniques can help streamline the editing process, allowing creators to quickly and easily edit their VR content. AI-powered video enhancement tools can also be used to improve the quality of VR videos, enhancing colors, reducing noise, and increasing sharpness to create a more visually appealing experience for viewers.

AI can also play a role in live video streaming and production in virtual reality. By using AI algorithms to analyze live footage, content creators can quickly identify and correct any technical issues that may arise during a live stream.

The Ultimate Guide to AI in Video Production

AI can also be used to automate certain aspects of the production process, such as camera angles and transitions, allowing creators to focus on delivering high-quality content to their audience.

Overall, AI has the potential to revolutionize the way virtual reality video production is done. By leveraging AI-driven video analytics and audience insights, creators can better understand their audience and tailor their content to meet their preferences. AI-generated video content creation can also help streamline the content creation process, allowing creators to quickly produce high-quality VR videos. With AI in virtual reality video production, the possibilities are endless for creating immersive and engaging VR experiences for audiences around the world.

03

Chapter 3: AI in Live Video Streaming and Production

Real-time AI Applications

Real-time AI applications in video production have revolutionized the way content creators work. These cutting-edge technologies are being used in various stages of video production, from editing to post-production and even live streaming. By incorporating AI into their workflows, video producers can streamline processes, enhance the quality of their content, and engage with their audiences like never before.

One of the key areas where real-time AI applications shine is in video editing. AI-driven video editing techniques can automate tasks such as color correction, audio syncing, and even scene detection. This not only saves time for editors but also ensures a more consistent and professional look across all videos. With AI-powered video enhancement tools, producers can further improve the visual quality of their content by upscaling resolution, removing noise, and enhancing colors.

The Ultimate Guide to AI in Video Production

In virtual reality video production, AI applications play a crucial role in creating immersive experiences for viewers. By analyzing user behavior and preferences, AI algorithms can personalize virtual reality content to cater to individual tastes. This level of customization enhances user engagement and provides a more interactive and dynamic viewing experience. AI in live video streaming and production is another area where real-time applications are making a significant impact. By using AI-driven analytics, producers can monitor audience reactions in real-time and adjust their content accordingly to maximize viewer engagement.

AI-generated video content creation is another exciting development in the field of video production. By using natural language processing and machine learning algorithms, AI can generate scripts, storyboard ideas, and even edit videos automatically. This not only speeds up the content creation process but also opens up new possibilities for storytelling and creativity. In post-production workflows, AI-driven personalization tools can help producers tailor their content to specific audiences by analyzing viewer data and preferences. This level of personalization can lead to higher viewer retention rates and increased audience satisfaction.

Overall, real-time AI applications have the potential to revolutionize the video production industry by streamlining workflows, enhancing content quality, and engaging audiences in new and innovative ways. By embracing these technologies, content creators can stay ahead of the curve and deliver cutting-edge video content that captivates viewers and drives success in today's competitive digital landscape.

Enhancing Live Video Production with AI Technology

Live video production has undergone significant advancements in recent years, thanks to the integration of artificial intelligence (AI) technology. AI has revolutionized the way live video content is created, produced, and streamed, allowing for more personalized and interactive experiences for viewers. In this subchapter, we will explore how AI is enhancing live video production and revolutionizing the industry.

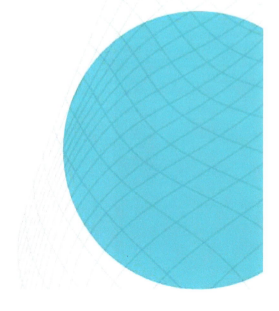

One of the key ways AI is transforming live video production is through AI-driven video editing techniques. AI algorithms can analyze footage in real-time, automatically selecting the best shots, enhancing audio quality, and even adding special effects. This not only streamlines the editing process but also ensures a more professional and polished final product.

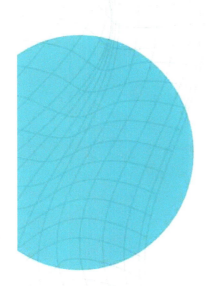

AI-powered video enhancement tools are also making a significant impact on live video production. These tools can automatically adjust lighting, colors, and even remove background noise, resulting in higher-quality video content. Additionally, AI algorithms can identify and correct errors in real-time, ensuring a seamless and error-free live stream.

Furthermore, AI applications in virtual reality video production are pushing the boundaries of what is possible in live video production. AI algorithms can create immersive virtual reality experiences, allowing viewers to interact with the content in real-time. This level of interactivity enhances viewer engagement and provides a more personalized viewing experience.

In addition, AI in live video streaming and production is revolutionizing how content is delivered to audiences. AI algorithms can analyze viewer behavior and preferences, automatically adjusting the content in real-time to cater to individual preferences. This level of personalization ensures that viewers are engaged and interested in the content being presented.

Overall, the integration of AI technology in live video production is transforming the industry and pushing the boundaries of what is possible. From AI-driven video editing techniques to AI applications in virtual reality video production, AI is enhancing the quality, interactivity, and personalization of live video content. As technology continues to evolve, the possibilities for AI in live video production are endless, making it an exciting time for those involved in the industry.

Case Studies and Success Stories

In this subchapter of "The Ultimate Guide to AI in Video Production," we will delve into real-world examples of how AI is being used in the industry to revolutionize video production processes. These case studies and success stories showcase the power of AI in transforming the way videos are created, edited, and distributed. Whether you are a seasoned professional or just starting out in the field, these examples will inspire you to explore the possibilities of AI in video production.

One of the most compelling case studies is the use of AI-driven video editing techniques by renowned production houses. By harnessing the power of AI algorithms, editors can automate tedious tasks such as color correction, audio syncing, and even script analysis. This not only speeds up the editing process but also ensures a more consistent and high-quality output. With AI-powered video enhancement tools, filmmakers can easily enhance the visual and audio quality of their videos, making them more engaging and professional-looking.

Another fascinating application of AI in video production is in virtual reality (VR) video production. By using AI algorithms to analyze and stitch together multiple camera angles, filmmakers can create immersive VR experiences that transport viewers to new and exciting worlds. This technology has been used in various industries, from gaming and entertainment to education and training, showcasing the versatility of AI in video production.

In the realm of live video streaming and production, AI-driven tools are being used to enhance the viewer experience in real-time. By analyzing viewer behavior and preferences, AI algorithms can automatically adjust camera angles, audio levels, and even lighting to create a more engaging and personalized viewing experience. This level of personalization not only keeps viewers engaged but also helps content creators attract and retain a larger audience.

The Ultimate Guide to AI in Video Production

Finally, AI-driven video analytics and audience insights are revolutionizing the way content creators understand and engage with their viewers. By analyzing viewer behavior, preferences, and engagement metrics, AI algorithms can provide valuable insights that help creators tailor their content to better meet the needs and interests of their audience. This data-driven approach not only improves content quality but also helps creators increase viewer engagement and retention.

Overall, these case studies and success stories demonstrate the transformative power of AI in video production. Whether you are a filmmaker, content creator, or industry professional, incorporating AI-driven techniques and tools into your workflow can help you create more engaging, high-quality videos that resonate with your audience. The possibilities are endless, and the future of AI in video production is bright.

04

Chapter 4: AI-driven Video Analytics and Audience Insights

How AI is Transforming Audience Engagement

In today's digital age, audience engagement has become a key focus for content creators and marketers looking to capture the attention of their target viewers. With the rise of Artificial Intelligence (AI) technology, the way in which audiences interact with video content has been transformed in ways that were previously unimaginable. This subchapter will delve into how AI is revolutionizing audience engagement in the realm of video production, offering insights and strategies for those looking to leverage this cutting-edge technology.

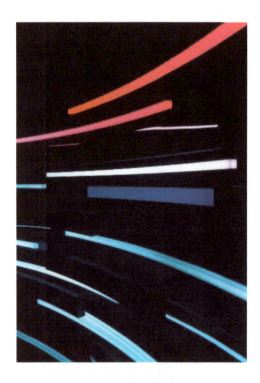

One of the most significant ways in which AI is transforming audience engagement is through its ability to analyze viewer behavior and preferences. By utilizing AI-driven video analytics tools, content creators can gain valuable insights into how their audience interacts with their content, allowing them to tailor their videos to better meet the needs and interests of their viewers. This data-driven approach to content creation enables creators to deliver more personalized and engaging video experiences, ultimately leading to increased viewer satisfaction and retention.

Furthermore, AI-powered video enhancement tools are revolutionizing the way in which videos are produced and edited. These tools leverage machine learning algorithms to automatically enhance video quality, adjust colors, and optimize audio, resulting in professional-looking videos that are sure to captivate audiences. By streamlining the editing process and improving the overall quality of video content, AI-driven editing tools are enabling creators to produce more engaging and visually appealing videos that resonate with their audience.

The Ultimate Guide to AI in Video Production

In addition to enhancing the production and editing process, AI is also playing a crucial role in revolutionizing audience engagement in virtual reality (VR) video production. By leveraging AI applications in VR video production, creators are able to deliver immersive and interactive experiences that transport viewers to new and exciting worlds. From dynamic storytelling to personalized experiences, AI is enabling creators to push the boundaries of traditional video production and engage audiences in ways that were previously thought impossible.

Overall, the integration of AI technology in video production is opening up a world of possibilities for content creators looking to engage their audience in new and innovative ways. From personalized content recommendations to immersive VR experiences, AI is transforming the landscape of audience engagement and offering exciting opportunities for those willing to embrace this cutting-edge technology. By staying informed and leveraging the latest AI-driven tools and techniques, content creators can create captivating videos that resonate with their audience and drive meaningful connections in today's digital world.

Harnessing Data for Better Video Performance

Harnessing data for better video performance is a crucial aspect of utilizing AI in video production. By leveraging data-driven insights, video creators can optimize their content for maximum impact and engagement. In this subchapter, we will explore how AI technologies can help improve video performance through data analysis and optimization techniques.

One of the key ways AI can help enhance video performance is through the use of AI-driven video editing techniques. These advanced algorithms can analyze video content and automatically make edits to improve the overall quality and appeal of the video. By utilizing AI-powered editing tools, video creators can save time and resources while still producing high-quality content.

Additionally, AI-powered video enhancement tools can help improve the visual and audio quality of videos. These tools can automatically adjust lighting, color, sound, and other elements to ensure that the final product is of the highest quality. By harnessing the power of AI, video creators can enhance their videos in ways that were previously not possible.

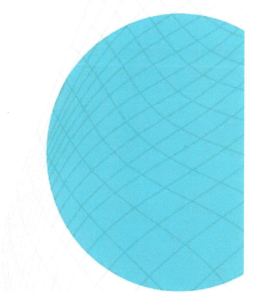

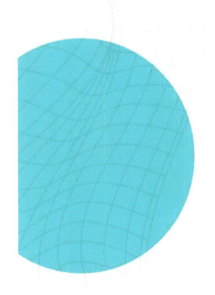

AI applications in virtual reality video production are also becoming increasingly popular. By using AI algorithms to analyze user behavior and preferences, video creators can optimize their VR content for maximum engagement. AI can help enhance the immersive experience of VR videos, making them more compelling and memorable for viewers.

Furthermore, AI-driven video analytics and audience insights can provide valuable data that can help video creators improve their content and reach a wider audience. By analyzing viewer behavior and preferences, video creators can tailor their content to better suit the needs and interests of their target audience. This data-driven approach can lead to higher engagement and more successful video campaigns.

Predictive Analytics and Trends in Video Production

The Ultimate Guide to AI in Video Production

In the world of video production, staying ahead of trends and leveraging cutting-edge technology is essential to creating high-quality content that captivates audiences. One of the most exciting developments in recent years is the use of predictive analytics in video production. Predictive analytics involves using data and algorithms to forecast future trends and behaviors, allowing video producers to make informed decisions about content creation and distribution.

By harnessing the power of predictive analytics, video producers can gain valuable insights into audience preferences and behavior. This information can be used to tailor content to specific demographics, optimize distribution strategies, and maximize engagement. For people that want to learn all there is to know regarding AI and Video Production, understanding how predictive analytics can be applied to video production is essential for staying competitive in the industry.

AI-driven video editing techniques have revolutionized the way videos are created, allowing producers to streamline workflows and enhance the overall quality of their content. From automated editing tools that can cut together footage in seconds to AI-powered color correction and sound editing software, AI is transforming the way videos are produced. By learning how to leverage these tools effectively, video producers can save time, improve efficiency, and create visually stunning content that resonates with audiences.

The Ultimate Guide to AI in Video Production

AI-powered video enhancement tools are another game-changer in the world of video production. These tools use advanced algorithms to analyze and enhance video quality, from upscaling resolution to removing background noise and enhancing colors. For those looking to create professional-looking videos without the need for expensive equipment or technical expertise, AI-powered video enhancement tools are a must-have in their toolkit.

As the demand for immersive content continues to grow, AI applications in virtual reality video production are becoming increasingly important. Virtual reality (VR) technology allows viewers to experience videos in a 360-degree environment, creating a truly immersive viewing experience. By using AI to enhance VR content, video producers can create lifelike environments, realistic animations, and interactive experiences that engage and captivate audiences like never before. For those looking to break into the world of VR video production, understanding how AI can be used to enhance and optimize VR content is essential for success.

05

Chapter 5: AI-generated Video Content Creation

The Ultimate Guide to AI in Video Production

Automating the Content Creation Process

Automating the content creation process is a game-changer in the world of video production. With the advancement of AI technology, creators can now streamline their workflow and produce high-quality videos in a fraction of the time. In this subchapter, we will explore the various ways in which AI can be utilized to automate the content creation process and revolutionize the way videos are produced.

One of the key benefits of using AI in content creation is its ability to generate personalized and engaging videos at scale. AI-driven video editing techniques can analyze data such as viewer preferences, demographics, and engagement metrics to automatically create videos that resonate with the target audience. This level of personalization not only increases viewer engagement but also saves creators valuable time and resources.

AI-powered video enhancement tools are another essential component of automating the content creation process. These tools use machine learning algorithms to automatically enhance video quality, adjust colors, and optimize audio levels. By utilizing these tools, creators can ensure that their videos are of the highest quality without the need for manual intervention.

In addition to enhancing video quality, AI applications in virtual reality video production have also revolutionized the way immersive experiences are created. AI algorithms can analyze user interactions and behaviors within virtual reality environments to automatically generate dynamic and engaging content. This level of automation not only saves time but also allows creators to focus on creating unique and interactive experiences for their audiences.

Furthermore, AI in live video streaming and production has enabled real-time data analysis and audience insights to enhance the viewer experience. By utilizing AI-driven video analytics, creators can track viewer engagement, sentiment, and behavior to make informed decisions on the fly. This level of automation not only improves the quality of live streams but also allows creators to adjust their content in real-time based on audience feedback.

Overall, automating the content creation process through AI-driven tools and techniques is essential for staying competitive in the ever-evolving world of video production. Whether it be generating personalized videos, enhancing video quality, creating immersive virtual reality experiences, or analyzing audience insights, AI has the potential to revolutionize the way videos are produced.

By embracing AI technology, creators can streamline their workflow, save time and resources, and ultimately create engaging and impactful videos for their audiences.

Personalization and Customization with AI

Personalization and customization are key elements in today's video production landscape, and AI technology is revolutionizing the way content creators can tailor their videos to specific audiences.

Whether it's creating personalized recommendations for viewers or customizing video content based on user preferences, AI is playing a crucial role in delivering a more engaging and interactive experience for viewers.

One of the most common uses of AI in personalization and customization is through recommendation algorithms. These algorithms analyze user data, such as viewing history and preferences, to suggest relevant content that is likely to resonate with each individual viewer. By leveraging AI-driven recommendation systems, content creators can increase viewer engagement and retention, ultimately leading to higher levels of viewer satisfaction and loyalty.

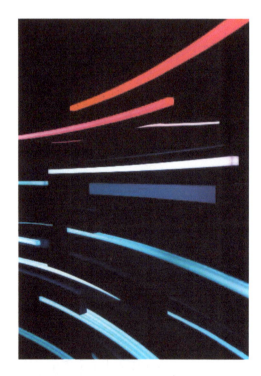

In addition to recommendation algorithms, AI is also being used to customize video content in real-time. Through the use of AI-powered editing tools, content creators can automatically adjust elements such as color grading, audio levels, and even scene transitions to better suit the preferences of each viewer. This level of customization not only enhances the viewing experience but also allows content creators to reach a wider audience by catering to individual tastes and preferences.

AI is also being utilized in post-production workflows to automate the process of video captioning and translation. By leveraging AI-driven tools, content creators can easily generate accurate captions and translations for their videos, making them more accessible to a global audience. This level of personalization and customization not only improves the overall viewing experience but also helps content creators reach a wider audience and increase engagement.

In conclusion, AI technology is revolutionizing the way content creators personalize and customize their videos to better suit the needs and preferences of their audience. From recommendation algorithms to real-time customization tools, AI is playing a crucial role in delivering a more engaging and interactive viewing experience. As AI continues to advance, we can expect to see even more innovative uses of AI in personalization and customization in the field of video production.

Challenges and Opportunities in AI Content Creation

In the realm of video production, artificial intelligence (AI) has revolutionized the way content is created, edited, and enhanced. However, along with the numerous opportunities that AI brings, there are also several challenges that content creators must navigate. This subchapter will explore the various challenges and opportunities in AI content creation, providing valuable insights for those looking to harness the power of AI in their video production endeavors.

The Ultimate Guide to AI in Video Production

One of the key challenges in AI content creation is ensuring the quality and authenticity of the content produced. While AI-powered tools can streamline the production process and enhance the visual appeal of videos, there is a risk of losing the human touch and creativity in the final product. Content creators must find a balance between leveraging AI technology and maintaining the unique voice and vision that sets their content apart.

Another challenge in AI content creation is the potential for bias and ethical concerns. AI algorithms are trained on large datasets, which can inadvertently perpetuate stereotypes or reinforce existing biases. Content creators must be mindful of the ethical implications of using AI in their production workflow and take steps to mitigate bias and ensure fair representation in their content.

Despite these challenges, there are numerous opportunities in AI content creation that can revolutionize the way videos are produced and consumed. AI-driven video editing techniques can automate repetitive tasks, saving time and resources for content creators. AI-powered video enhancement tools can improve the quality of videos, making them more visually appealing and engaging for audiences.

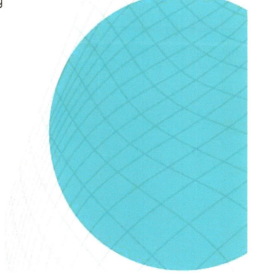

The Ultimate Guide to AI in Video Production

AI applications in virtual reality video production are also opening up new possibilities for immersive storytelling and interactive experiences. By harnessing the power of AI, content creators can create personalized and interactive videos that captivate audiences and drive engagement. AI-driven video analytics and audience insights provide valuable data that can inform content strategy and help creators optimize their videos for maximum impact.

Overall, the challenges and opportunities in AI content creation present a dynamic landscape for content creators to explore and innovate. By understanding the potential pitfalls and benefits of using AI in video production, creators can leverage this powerful technology to create compelling and impactful content that resonates with audiences in new and exciting ways.

06

Chapter 6: AI in Post-production Workflows

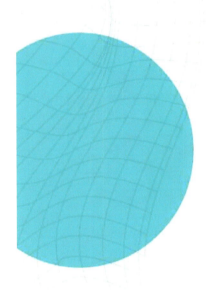

Streamlining Post-production Processes with AI

In the world of video production, post-production processes can often be time-consuming and labor-intensive. However, with the advancements in artificial intelligence technology, these processes can now be streamlined and made more efficient than ever before. AI has the ability to automate tasks, analyze data, and make predictions that can greatly improve the overall quality and efficiency of post-production workflows.

One of the key ways that AI is revolutionizing post-production processes is through AI-driven video editing techniques. These techniques use algorithms to analyze and edit video footage, making it easier for editors to make quick and precise edits. AI can also be used to automatically generate transitions, color correct footage, and even add special effects, saving editors valuable time and resources.

AI-powered video enhancement tools are another important aspect of streamlining post-production processes. These tools use AI algorithms to enhance the quality of video footage, improving things like color, sharpness, and stability. By using AI-powered enhancement tools, editors can quickly and easily improve the overall look and feel of their videos without having to spend hours manually adjusting settings.

In addition to video editing and enhancement, AI is also being used in virtual reality video production to create more immersive and interactive experiences. AI algorithms can analyze data from VR cameras to create 3D models, add special effects, and even predict user behavior. This allows VR producers to create more engaging content that is tailored to their audience's preferences.

Overall, AI is transforming the way post-production processes are handled in the world of video production. By using AI-driven tools and techniques, editors can streamline their workflows, improve the quality of their videos, and create more engaging and immersive content. As AI technology continues to advance, the possibilities for post-production processes in video production are endless.

Enhancing Visual Effects and Editing with AI

In the world of video production, visual effects and editing play a crucial role in creating captivating and engaging content. With the advancements in artificial intelligence (AI) technology, filmmakers and video producers now have access to a wide range of AI-driven tools and techniques that can greatly enhance the visual quality of their videos. In this chapter, we will explore how AI is revolutionizing the way visual effects and editing are done in the industry.

One of the key benefits of using AI in video production is the ability to automate and streamline the editing process. AI-powered video editing tools can analyze footage, identify key moments, and even suggest creative editing choices to enhance the overall look and feel of the video. This not only saves time for video editors, but also allows for more creative freedom and experimentation in the editing process.

AI-powered video enhancement tools are another game-changer in the industry. These tools use machine learning algorithms to automatically enhance the visual quality of videos by adjusting colors, contrast, and sharpness. This can result in videos that look more professional and polished, without the need for manual editing. From color grading to image stabilization, AI-driven video enhancement tools are becoming increasingly popular among video producers looking to improve the overall quality of their content.

AI applications in virtual reality (VR) video production are also on the rise. Virtual reality videos require complex editing and post-production techniques to create immersive and realistic experiences for viewers. AI can help streamline this process by automating tasks such as stitching together multiple video clips, adding special effects, and enhancing the overall visual quality of the VR experience.

In addition to enhancing visual effects and editing, AI is also being used in live video streaming and production. AI-driven tools can analyze real-time data to improve video quality, optimize streaming performance, and even personalize the viewing experience for individual viewers. This level of automation and personalization is unprecedented in the industry, and is revolutionizing the way live video content is produced and delivered to audiences.

Overall, AI is transforming the way visual effects and editing are done in video production. From automating editing tasks to enhancing visual quality, AI-driven tools and techniques are making it easier than ever for video producers to create high-quality, engaging content. As AI continues to evolve and improve, the possibilities for enhancing visual effects and editing in video production are endless.

The Future of Post-production in a AI-driven World

The future of post-production in an AI-driven world is a topic that is gaining increasing attention in the video production industry. As artificial intelligence continues to advance, it is revolutionizing the way post-production work is done. In this subchapter, we will explore how AI is transforming the post-production process and what it means for the future of video production.

One of the key advancements in AI-driven post-production is the use of machine learning algorithms to automate tasks that were previously time-consuming and labor-intensive. AI-powered video editing techniques are making it easier for editors to quickly and efficiently edit footage, saving both time and money. These algorithms can analyze footage and make suggestions for cuts, transitions, and effects, speeding up the editing process and improving overall quality.

AI-powered video enhancement tools are also playing a major role in the future of post-production. These tools use AI algorithms to automatically enhance video quality, adjust colors, and improve audio. This not only saves time for editors but also ensures a higher quality final product.

By leveraging AI-powered enhancement tools, video producers can create professional-looking videos with minimal effort.

AI applications are also being used in virtual reality video production to create immersive experiences for viewers. By using AI algorithms to analyze and process VR footage, producers can create interactive and engaging content that draws viewers in. AI is helping to push the boundaries of what is possible in VR video production, opening up new possibilities for storytelling and audience engagement.

In addition to the advancements in virtual reality, AI is also being used in live video streaming and production to improve the viewer experience. AI-driven video analytics and audience insights are providing producers with valuable data on viewer behavior, preferences, and engagement levels. This data can be used to optimize live streams, tailor content to specific audiences, and improve overall production quality.

Overall, the future of post-production in an AI-driven world is full of exciting possibilities. From AI-generated video content creation to AI in post-production workflows, the use of artificial intelligence is transforming the way videos are produced and consumed. By staying informed and embracing these advancements, video producers can stay ahead of the curve and create cutting-edge content that captivates audiences.

07

Chapter 7: AI-driven Personalization in Video Production

Customizing Video Content for Target Audiences

In the world of video production, one of the most powerful tools at our disposal is artificial intelligence. AI has revolutionized the way we create and distribute video content, allowing us to tailor our messages to specific target audiences with incredible precision. In this subchapter, we will explore the ways in which AI can be used to customize video content for different demographic groups, ensuring that our messages resonate with the people we are trying to reach.

One of the key benefits of using AI to customize video content is the ability to analyze data on a massive scale. By collecting and analyzing information on viewer preferences, demographics, and behaviors, AI can help us better understand our target audiences and create video content that speaks directly to their interests and needs. This data-driven approach allows us to create more relevant and engaging video content, increasing the likelihood that our messages will resonate with our intended viewers.

The Ultimate Guide to AI in Video Production

AI-driven video editing techniques are another powerful tool for customizing video content. By using machine learning algorithms to analyze and edit video footage, we can create personalized videos that are tailored to the preferences of our target audiences. Whether we are adjusting the color palette, editing the length of a video, or adding special effects, AI can help us create videos that are perfectly suited to the tastes of our viewers.

AI-powered video enhancement tools can also be used to customize video content for different target audiences. These tools can automatically adjust the lighting, color balance, and sound quality of a video, ensuring that it looks and sounds its best for each viewer. By using AI to enhance our videos, we can create a more professional and polished final product that will appeal to a wider range of audiences.

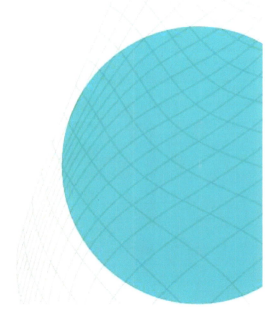

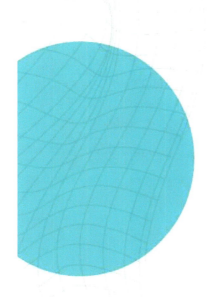

In conclusion, AI offers a wide range of tools and techniques for customizing video content for target audiences. By leveraging the power of machine learning and data analysis, we can create personalized videos that speak directly to the interests and needs of our viewers. Whether we are editing video footage, enhancing video quality, or analyzing audience data, AI can help us create more engaging and effective video content that will resonate with our target audiences. By understanding and utilizing these AI-driven techniques, we can take our video production skills to the next level and create content that truly stands out in a crowded digital landscape.

Creating Personalized Video Experiences

The Ultimate Guide to AI in Video Production

Creating personalized video experiences is an essential aspect of modern video production, as it allows content creators to tailor their videos to the specific interests and preferences of their audience. With the advancements in artificial intelligence (AI) technology, it has become easier than ever to create personalized video experiences that resonate with viewers on a deeper level.

One of the key ways AI is used to create personalized video experiences is through AI-driven video editing techniques. These techniques use algorithms to analyze the content of a video and make intelligent editing decisions based on factors such as pacing, tone, and visual style. By utilizing AI-powered editing tools, content creators can streamline the editing process and produce videos that are more engaging and impactful.

In addition to editing, AI-powered video enhancement tools are also instrumental in creating personalized video experiences. These tools use machine learning algorithms to automatically enhance the quality of video footage, such as improving color balance, reducing noise, and enhancing clarity. By using AI-powered enhancement tools, content creators can ensure that their videos look polished and professional, which ultimately leads to a more personalized viewing experience for the audience.

AI applications in virtual reality video production have also revolutionized the way personalized video experiences are created. By leveraging AI technology, content creators can create immersive VR experiences that respond to the viewer's actions and preferences in real-time. This level of interactivity allows for a truly personalized viewing experience, as viewers can explore virtual environments and engage with content in a way that is unique to them.

Overall, AI-driven personalization in video production is transforming the way content is created and consumed. By harnessing the power of AI technologies, content creators can create videos that are tailored to the individual preferences of their audience, leading to more engaging and impactful content. Whether it's through editing, enhancement, virtual reality, or other applications, AI is revolutionizing the world of video production and paving the way for truly personalized video experiences.

Implementing AI-driven Personalization Strategies

Personalization in video production has become increasingly important as audiences expect content tailored to their preferences and interests. With the help of artificial intelligence (AI), creators can now create personalized video experiences that resonate with viewers on a deeper level. In this subchapter, we will explore how AI-driven personalization strategies are revolutionizing the way videos are produced and consumed.

One of the key ways AI is used for personalization in video production is through recommendation algorithms. These algorithms analyze user data such as viewing history, preferences, and behavior to suggest content that is likely to be of interest to the viewer. By leveraging AI-powered recommendation systems, video creators can increase engagement and retention rates by delivering relevant content to their audience.

Another aspect of AI-driven personalization in video production is dynamic content generation. AI algorithms can analyze viewer data in real-time to create personalized video content on the fly. This allows creators to deliver unique and tailored experiences to each viewer, increasing the likelihood of viewer satisfaction and engagement.

Furthermore, AI-driven personalization strategies can also be applied to video editing and enhancement tools. AI-powered tools can automatically analyze and edit videos based on viewer preferences, creating personalized experiences that resonate with each individual viewer. Additionally, AI-powered video enhancement tools can improve video quality, color correction, and visual effects to create a more engaging and personalized viewing experience.

In conclusion, implementing AI-driven personalization strategies in video production can significantly enhance the viewer experience and increase audience engagement. By leveraging AI-powered recommendation algorithms, dynamic content generation, and personalized video editing tools, creators can deliver content that is tailored to the preferences and interests of their audience.

The Ultimate Guide to AI in Video Production

As technology continues to advance, the possibilities for AI-driven personalization in video production are endless, offering creators the opportunity to create truly unique and engaging video content for their viewers.

08

Chapter 8: AI in Automated Video Captioning and Translation

Improving Accessibility with AI-driven Captioning

One of the most significant benefits of using AI in video production is the ability to improve accessibility through AI-driven captioning. Captioning is essential for individuals who are deaf or hard of hearing, as well as those who speak different languages or have difficulty understanding spoken language. By leveraging AI technology, video producers can automatically generate accurate and synchronized captions for their content, making it more inclusive and accessible to a wider audience.

AI-driven captioning uses advanced speech recognition and natural language processing algorithms to transcribe spoken words into text in real-time. This technology can accurately capture dialogue, background noise, and other audio elements, ensuring that the captions are both informative and contextually relevant. Additionally, AI can automatically synchronize captions with the video, making it easier for viewers to follow along and engage with the content.

In addition to improving accessibility, AI-driven captioning can also enhance the overall viewing experience for all audiences. By providing captions, video producers can make their content more engaging and immersive, as viewers can easily follow along with the dialogue and storyline. This can lead to increased viewer retention and engagement, ultimately driving higher levels of viewer satisfaction and loyalty.

Furthermore, AI-driven captioning can help video producers save time and resources by automating the captioning process. Instead of manually transcribing and synchronizing captions, producers can rely on AI technology to generate accurate and high-quality captions quickly and efficiently. This allows producers to focus on other aspects of video production, such as editing and post-production, without sacrificing the quality of their captions.

Overall, AI-driven captioning is a powerful tool for improving accessibility, enhancing the viewing experience, and streamlining the video production process. By leveraging AI technology, video producers can make their content more inclusive, engaging, and efficient, ultimately leading to greater success in the competitive landscape of video production.

Translating Videos for Global Audiences

In today's globalized world, reaching audiences from diverse cultural backgrounds is more important than ever. With the help of artificial intelligence (AI), video producers can now easily translate their content to cater to viewers from all around the world. This subchapter will explore the various AI-driven techniques and tools available for translating videos for global audiences.

The Ultimate Guide to AI in Video Production

One of the most popular AI-driven video translation tools is automatic speech recognition (ASR) technology. ASR allows video producers to transcribe spoken dialogue in videos and then automatically translate it into different languages. This not only makes videos more accessible to non-native speakers but also enhances the overall viewing experience for global audiences.

Another powerful AI tool for translating videos is neural machine translation (NMT) technology. NMT uses deep learning algorithms to analyze and translate text in videos with higher accuracy and fluency compared to traditional machine translation methods. This technology enables video producers to create seamless multilingual content that resonates with viewers worldwide.

In addition to translating spoken dialogue, AI can also be used to translate on-screen text in videos. Optical character recognition (OCR) technology can identify and extract text from videos, which can then be translated into different languages using natural language processing (NLP) algorithms. This ensures that all textual information in videos is accessible and understandable to global audiences.

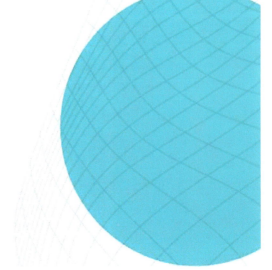

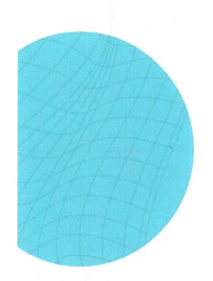

Moreover, AI-powered video editing tools can help streamline the translation process by automatically synchronizing translated audio and text with video footage. This not only saves time and effort for video producers but also ensures that the final translated content is of high quality and accurately reflects the original message.

Overall, the use of AI in translating videos for global audiences opens up endless possibilities for video producers to reach and engage with viewers from all corners of the world. By leveraging AI-driven techniques and tools, video producers can create multilingual content that is not only culturally relevant but also resonates with global audiences on a personal level.

The Impact of AI on Video Localization

The Ultimate Guide to AI in Video Production

Video localization is the process of adapting audiovisual content to a specific target audience in a different region or language. This process has traditionally been time-consuming and costly, requiring human translators and editors to manually transcribe, translate, and edit video content. However, with the advent of artificial intelligence (AI) technology, video localization has been revolutionized.

AI-powered video localization tools utilize machine learning algorithms to automatically transcribe, translate, and edit video content in real-time. These tools can accurately transcribe spoken dialogue, translate text, and even adjust subtitles to match the lip movements of the actors on screen. This not only saves time and money but also ensures a higher level of accuracy and consistency in the localization process.

One of the key benefits of AI in video localization is its ability to reach a global audience more effectively. By automatically translating video content into multiple languages, companies can expand their reach and connect with a wider audience. This can lead to increased viewership, engagement, and ultimately, revenue.

AI-powered video localization tools also provide a more personalized viewing experience for audiences. By analyzing viewer data and preferences, AI can automatically tailor video content to suit individual tastes and preferences. This level of personalization can enhance viewer engagement and retention, leading to a more loyal and satisfied audience.

The Ultimate Guide to AI in Video Production

Overall, the impact of AI on video localization is undeniable. With its ability to automate and streamline the localization process, AI is revolutionizing the way companies create and distribute video content to a global audience. By leveraging AI technology, companies can reach new markets, engage with audiences on a deeper level, and ultimately, drive success in the ever-evolving world of video production.

09

Chapter 9: AI in Interactive Video Production and Storytelling

Creating Immersive and Interactive Video Experiences

In today's digital age, creating immersive and interactive video experiences has become essential for engaging audiences and standing out in a crowded market. With the advancements in Artificial Intelligence (AI) technology, video production has been revolutionized, allowing for more personalized and interactive content creation. In this subchapter, we will explore how AI is transforming the way videos are produced and how you can leverage these tools to create captivating video experiences for your audience.

One of the key benefits of AI in video production is its ability to automate the editing process. AI-driven video editing techniques can help streamline the editing workflow, saving time and resources. By analyzing the content of the video, AI algorithms can make intelligent editing decisions, such as cutting out unnecessary footage or adding special effects, to enhance the overall quality of the video.

AI-powered video enhancement tools have also become increasingly popular in the industry. These tools use machine learning algorithms to automatically enhance video quality, adjust colors, and optimize audio levels. By incorporating these tools into your production process, you can ensure that your videos are visually appealing and professional-looking, without the need for manual editing.

The Ultimate Guide to AI in Video Production

In the realm of virtual reality video production, AI applications have opened up new possibilities for creating immersive experiences. AI algorithms can analyze user behavior and preferences to personalize virtual reality content, making it more engaging and interactive. By harnessing the power of AI in virtual reality video production, you can create unique and memorable experiences that will captivate your audience.

Another area where AI is making a significant impact is in live video streaming and production. AI-driven video analytics can provide valuable insights into audience behavior, allowing you to tailor your content in real-time to better engage viewers. Additionally, AI algorithms can automate tasks such as camera switching and live captioning, making live video production more efficient and seamless.

Overall, AI is revolutionizing the way videos are produced, from automated editing to personalized content creation. By embracing AI technology in your video production workflow, you can create immersive and interactive video experiences that will captivate your audience and set your content apart from the competition. Whether you are a beginner or an experienced professional, understanding AI-driven techniques and tools is essential for taking your video production to the next level.

Enhancing Storytelling with AI Technology

Enhancing storytelling with AI technology has revolutionized the video production industry, providing creators with powerful tools to bring their vision to life in exciting new ways. By leveraging artificial intelligence, filmmakers and content creators can now enhance their storytelling capabilities like never before.

One of the key ways AI technology enhances storytelling in video production is through AI-driven video editing techniques. These techniques allow editors to streamline the editing process, saving time and resources while ensuring a high-quality end product. With AI-powered tools, editors can easily cut, splice, and enhance footage with precision and efficiency, ultimately enhancing the overall storytelling experience for viewers.

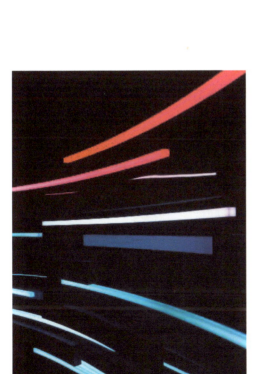

AI-powered video enhancement tools are another game-changer in the world of storytelling. These tools use advanced algorithms to improve video quality, enhance colors, and even remove unwanted elements from footage. By utilizing AI technology, creators can elevate the visual appeal of their videos, creating a more immersive and engaging experience for their audience.

In the realm of virtual reality video production, AI applications have opened up new possibilities for storytelling. By using AI algorithms to analyze user behavior and preferences, creators can tailor VR experiences to individual viewers, creating a more personalized and interactive storytelling experience. This level of customization allows creators to engage their audiences in a whole new way, making VR storytelling more captivating and immersive than ever before.

Overall, AI technology is transforming the way stories are told in video production. From automated video captioning and translation to personalized content creation, AI is empowering creators to push the boundaries of storytelling in exciting new ways. By embracing AI in all aspects of video production, creators can enhance their storytelling capabilities and captivate audiences like never before.

The Future of Interactive Video Production

As we look ahead to the future of interactive video production, it is clear that artificial intelligence (AI) will play a significant role in shaping the way videos are created, edited, and shared. With the advancements in AI technology, the possibilities for interactive video production are endless. AI-driven video editing techniques are already revolutionizing the way videos are edited, allowing for more efficient and creative workflows.

The Ultimate Guide to AI in Video Production

AI-powered video enhancement tools are also transforming the way videos are produced, allowing for automated color correction, noise reduction, and image stabilization. These tools are making it easier than ever to create high-quality videos with minimal effort. Additionally, AI applications in virtual reality video production are opening up new possibilities for immersive storytelling and interactive experiences.

In the realm of live video streaming and production, AI is being used to enhance the viewer experience by providing real-time analytics and audience insights. This allows content creators to tailor their videos to their audience's preferences and interests, creating a more engaging and personalized viewing experience. AI-driven video analytics are also providing valuable data on viewer behavior, helping content creators better understand their audience and optimize their content for maximum engagement.

AI-generated video content creation is another exciting development in the world of interactive video production. With AI algorithms capable of generating realistic videos from scratch, content creators can now produce high-quality videos in a fraction of the time it would take using traditional methods. This opens up new possibilities for creating personalized and engaging video content at scale.

As we continue to explore the potential of AI in video production, the possibilities for interactive video production and storytelling are truly limitless. From automated video captioning and translation to personalized video production workflows, AI is reshaping the way videos are created and consumed. By staying informed and embracing the latest AI technologies, content creators can stay ahead of the curve and create truly innovative and engaging video content for their audiences.

10

Chapter 10: Conclusion

Recap of Key Concepts

In this subchapter, we will provide a recap of the key concepts discussed in this book, "The Ultimate Guide to AI in Video Production." For people that want to learn all there is to know regarding AI and Video Production, this book offers a comprehensive guide on AI-driven video editing techniques, AI-powered video enhancement tools, AI applications in virtual reality video production, AI in live video streaming and production, AI-driven video analytics and audience insights, AI-generated video content creation, AI in post-production workflows, AI-driven personalization in video production, AI in automated video captioning and translation, and AI in interactive video production and storytelling.

First and foremost, we explored the various ways in which AI is revolutionizing video production through advanced editing techniques. From automatic scene detection to intelligent color correction, AI-driven video editing tools are streamlining the post-production process and helping creators bring their vision to life more efficiently than ever before.

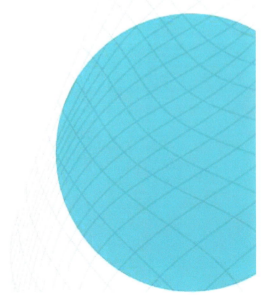

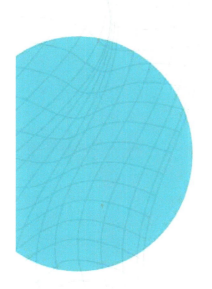

Next, we delved into the world of AI-powered video enhancement tools, which are making it possible to improve the quality of video footage in ways that were previously unimaginable. Whether it's reducing noise, enhancing resolution, or even transforming 2D footage into 3D, AI is enabling filmmakers to achieve stunning results with minimal effort.

We also discussed the exciting applications of AI in virtual reality video production, where intelligent algorithms are being used to create immersive experiences that blur the line between reality and fiction. By leveraging AI technology, creators can build interactive and dynamic VR worlds that captivate audiences and transport them to new and exciting realms.

Furthermore, we explored the role of AI in live video streaming and production, where real-time analytics and automated processes are enabling broadcasters to deliver high-quality content to viewers around the globe with unprecedented speed and accuracy. With AI-driven tools at their disposal, live streamers can enhance their productions, engage their audiences, and optimize their workflows for maximum impact.

Lastly, we examined the power of AI-driven video analytics and audience insights, which are empowering creators to better understand their viewers and tailor their content to meet their needs and preferences. By harnessing the power of AI, video producers can gain valuable insights into viewer behavior, engagement patterns, and content performance, allowing them to optimize their strategies and drive greater success in the competitive world of video production.

Looking Ahead: Trends and Developments in AI Video Production

As technology continues to advance at a rapid pace, the world of video production is no exception. AI is playing an increasingly important role in revolutionizing the way videos are created, edited, and enhanced. In this subchapter, we will explore some of the latest trends and developments in AI video production that are shaping the future of the industry.

One of the most exciting trends in AI video production is the emergence of AI-driven video editing techniques. These techniques use machine learning algorithms to analyze and edit video footage automatically, saving time and effort for video editors. AI-powered video enhancement tools are also becoming more sophisticated, allowing users to enhance the quality of their videos with just a few clicks.

Another trend to watch out for is the integration of AI applications in virtual reality video production. AI algorithms can be used to create realistic virtual environments and characters, enhancing the immersive experience for viewers. AI is also making waves in live video streaming and production, with algorithms that can automatically adjust camera angles and lighting to create a professional-looking broadcast.

AI-driven video analytics and audience insights are helping creators understand their viewers better than ever before. By analyzing viewer behavior and preferences, AI can help creators tailor their content to better engage their audience. AI-generated video content creation is another exciting development, with algorithms that can generate video scripts and storyboards based on a set of parameters.

In the realm of post-production workflows, AI is streamlining the editing process by automating tasks such as color correction, audio editing, and visual effects. AI-driven personalization in video production is also on the rise, with algorithms that can create personalized video content for individual viewers. Lastly, AI is making strides in automated video captioning and translation, making videos more accessible to audiences around the world. With these trends and developments in AI video production, the future of the industry looks brighter than ever.

Resources for Further Learning and Exploration

The Ultimate Guide to AI in Video Production

For people that want to learn all there is to know regarding AI and Video Production, there are a plethora of resources available for further learning and exploration in this exciting field. Whether you are interested in comprehensive guides on AI in video production, AI-driven video editing techniques, AI-powered video enhancement tools, AI applications in virtual reality video production, AI in live video streaming and production, AI-driven video analytics and audience insights, AI-generated video content creation, AI in post-production workflows, AI-driven personalization in video production, AI in automated video captioning and translation, or AI in interactive video production and storytelling, there are resources tailored to your specific interests.

One great resource for further learning on AI in video production is online courses and tutorials. Websites like Coursera, Udemy, and LinkedIn Learning offer a wide range of courses that cover various aspects of AI in video production, from beginner to advanced levels. These courses often include hands-on projects and assignments that allow you to apply what you have learned in a practical setting.

Another valuable resource for those looking to delve deeper into the world of AI in video production is books and research papers. There are many books written by experts in the field that provide in-depth insights into the latest developments and trends in AI technology as it relates to video production.

Research papers published in academic journals are also a great way to stay up-to-date on cutting-edge research in this field.

Attending conferences and workshops is another excellent way to expand your knowledge and network with other professionals in the field of AI and video production. These events often feature keynote speakers, panel discussions, and hands-on workshops that cover a wide range of topics related to AI technology in video production. They also provide a great opportunity to meet and collaborate with like-minded individuals who share your passion for this exciting industry.

Finally, online forums and communities dedicated to AI in video production are a valuable resource for connecting with other professionals and enthusiasts in the field. Websites like Reddit, Stack Exchange, and LinkedIn groups provide a platform for asking questions, sharing ideas, and networking with others who are interested in AI technology in video production.

The Ultimate Guide to AI in Video Production

These communities can be a great source of inspiration and collaboration as you continue your journey of learning and exploration in this dynamic field.